CHARLIE BROWN'S 'CYCLOPEDIA

Super Questions and Answers and Amazing Facts

Featuring Machines and How They Work

Volume 13

Based on the Charles M. Schulz Characters

Funk & Wagnalls, Inc.

Photograph and Illustration Credits: American Petroleum Institute, 587; Bergen Record, 610, 611; The Bettman Archive, Inc., 622; Black Star/© 1979 Ricardo Ferro, 614; Consumer & Educational Affairs Dept., Coats & Clark, Inc., 620; Colonial Williamsburg Photograph, 604; Culver Pictures, Inc., 609; Terry Flanagan, 593; Rita Ford Music Boxes, New York, 596; Ford Motor Company, 623; © Fundamental Photographs, 596; © Larry Dale Gordon 1976/The Image Bank, x; © Farrell Grehan 1972/Photo Researchers, Inc., x; Lares Manufacturing Co., Inc., 586; Richard Megna/Fundamental Photographs, 590; Richard Megna/Fundamental Photographs © 1980, 580; The Metropolitan Museum of Art, Gift of Mary J. Kingsland, 1906, 598; The Metropolitan Museum of Art, Gift of I.N. Phelps Stokes, Edward S. Hawes, Alice Mary Hawes, Marion Augusta Hawes, 1937, 619; New Hampshire Ball Bearings, Inc., 589; Nova Scotia Department of Government Services Information Services Photo, 624; Otis Elevator Company, 616; Kip Peticolas/Fundamental Photographs © 1980, 613; The Singer Company, 618, 619; Stanley Tools, Division of the Stanley Works, 585; Yale University Art Gallery, Gift of George Hoadly, Yale 1801, 622.

15   14   13   12   11

A large part of this volume was previously published in *Charlie Brown's Fifth Super Book of Questions and Answers.*

Introduction

Welcome to volume 13 of *Charlie Brown's 'Cyclopedia*! Have you ever wondered how a zipper works, or what makes springs bouncy, or why grandfather clocks are tall? Charlie Brown and the rest of the *Peanuts* gang are here to help you find the answers to these questions and many more about machines and how they work. Have fun!

Machines and How They Work

What is a machine?

A machine is an object that makes hard work easier or slow work faster. It gives the person using it greater speed or greater force. ("Force" means a push or pull.) A machine is usually made up of a few connected parts. A vacuum cleaner is a machine that makes housecleaning easy and fast. A car is a machine that lets people move much faster than they could by walking. A telephone is a machine that makes it possible to talk to someone far away.

Do all machines have motors?

No. There are many machines that have no motors. The power for doing work with many of these machines comes from people's muscles. A scissors, a shovel, a saw, a broom, a screwdriver, a corkscrew, a bottle opener, and even a fly swatter are machines without motors. And so is a seesaw.

How can a seesaw be a machine?

A seesaw is a machine because it helps to do work—the work of lifting another person. In fact, with a seesaw, you can lift a person heavier than you are (if the heavier person moves forward on the seesaw). You certainly couldn't do that without the help of a machine! The seesaw makes it possible for you to use greater force than you could without it.

A seesaw is a kind of machine called a lever (LEV-ur). A lever is a stiff bar that turns on a point. This point is called a fulcrum (FULL-krum). When a seesaw is used by two people who weigh about the same, its fulcrum is right around the center of the bar.

What other machine can you find in a playground?

A slide. A slide is a kind of machine called an inclined plane. A plane is a flat surface. An incline is a slope or tilt. An inclined plane is a tilted flat surface. It makes moving things between high places and low places easier. On a slide, the thing that moves down easily is you!

An inclined plane something like a slide is used to unload boxes from a truck. Often this machine has little wheels on it. The wheels make the boxes move more quickly down the tilted plane.

Airplanes got their name from the planes, or flat surfaces, that hold them up in the air. These flat surfaces are the wings!

Who invented the wheel?

Nobody knows. But it was one of the most useful inventions ever made.

How are wheels used?

Wheels help people and things move around on land. Cars and trains could not work if they didn't have wheels on which to move. Neither could bicycles, skateboards, shopping carts, baby carriages, and lots of other things. Wheels sometimes connect motors to machines. In this way motors, rather than people, can supply the energy to make the machines work. Some machines that use wheels are a doorknob, a water faucet, an eggbeater, and a drill.

latch

axle

How does a doorknob work?

A doorknob is a wheel attached to a rod called an axle. The axle goes through the door. At the other end of the axle is another doorknob. When you turn one of the doorknobs, it turns the axle. The axle pushes a bar that's connected to the latch. The latch is the piece of metal that sticks out of the edge of the door. It fits into a little hole in the wall when the door is closed. The latch is what keeps the door from opening until you turn the knob. When you close the door, a spring makes the latch pop into the hole in the wall. The same spring also does another job. It makes the doorknob go back into place after you turn the knob and let go.

CLOMP!

WHY HE NEEDS AN AUTOMATIC DOOR-OPENER IS BEYOND ME

SCHULZ

How does a faucet work?

A faucet is attached to the end of a water pipe. It holds the water in the pipe until you decide to let some out. There is a hole between the water pipe and the spigot. This hole is stopped up by a plug. Turning the handle in one direction causes the plug to come partway out of the hole. Then water flows through. Turning the handle in the other direction puts the plug back in the hole. Then water can't leave the pipe. At the end of the plug is a piece of rubber called a washer. It makes the plug fit tightly in the hole. So the faucet doesn't drip when you turn it off.

The ancient Romans were using water faucets about 2,000 years ago!

Is a crank a grouchy person?

Yes. But the word "crank" has another meaning, too. On a machine, a crank is a bar or handle that you turn in order to make a wheel or axle turn. When the wheel or axle turns, the machine works. The pedals on a bicycle are cranks. When you pedal, the wheels turn and the bike moves. The handle you turn to make a car window go up and down also is a crank. So is the handle you turn on a fishing reel.

Why do people use a rod and reel for fishing?

To get their bait into deep water where the big fish are. When you fish from the edge of a lake or river, or from an ocean beach, you are far from the deep water. You need a fishing rod to help you throw your fishing line farther than your arm could alone. You also need a very long line. The reel stores the long line neatly and it keeps it from getting tangled. When you throw (or "cast," as fishermen say), the reel lets the line go out very far. When you catch a fish, the crank on the reel helps you to pull in the line quickly and easily.

Why is an eggbeater better than a fork for whipping cream?

You can whip cream faster with an eggbeater than you can with a fork. An eggbeater has a crank. When you turn the crank, it turns a gear. This gear is a wheel with little teeth on it. It pushes two smaller gears that are attached to the two beaters. As these three gears turn, their teeth hook onto each other and then unhook again. Each time the big gear goes around once, the little gears go around a few times. So do the beaters. This means the little gears are turning faster than the big gear. It also means that the beaters are spinning faster than you are turning the crank. An eggbeater helps you by changing slow cranking into fast beating.

What machine looks like an eggbeater?

One kind of hand drill. It has a crank and gears like an eggbeater. But instead of beaters, it has a chuck and a bit. The bit is the part of the drill that actually makes the holes. Some bits look a lot like wood screws. The chuck holds the bit in place.

When someone wants to drill a hole in wood, metal, or plastic, here is what must be done. The person drilling holds the bit against the proper spot and turns the handle. The handle turns the gears. The gears turn the chuck and the bit, creating a hole.

Hand drill

chuck —

bit —

585

Does a dentist's drill work like other kinds of drills?

A dentist's drill is really more like a file than like other drills. Dental drill bits are called burs. A bur is a tiny, rough ball on the end of a stick. When the bur spins around, it scrapes away little pieces of tooth. Years ago, dentists used drills that turned very slowly. That meant it took a long time to drill a cavity. And nobody likes to have his or her teeth drilled for a long time. Modern dentists use drills that spin the bur many thousands of times a minute. That's fast! And it means the dentist can finish drilling in a very short time. But such fast scraping against the tooth makes the drill and the tooth get hot. So they are cooled by water. It flows through holes in the drill onto the patient's tooth.

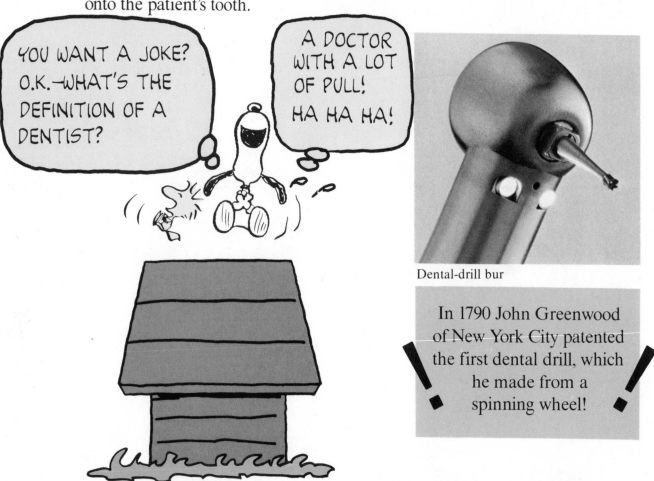

Dental-drill bur

In 1790 John Greenwood of New York City patented the first dental drill, which he made from a spinning wheel!

What do inventors do to machines when they patent them?

When inventors patent their machines, they get exclusive rights from their government to make and sell the machines. This means that no one is allowed to copy their machines. And no one else is allowed to make money from their ideas. In the United States of America, a patent lasts for 17 years. It cannot be renewed.

How are oil wells drilled?

Oil-well drills have to cut through rock to reach an underground pool of oil. Rock is very hard to cut. And often the hole has to be miles deep. Scraping on rock makes most drill bits wear out quickly and get dull. So, a special oil-well bit was designed to break the rock into little pieces. The bit has toothed wheels that look much like gears. The teeth are made of hardened metal. And sometimes they are diamond tipped for extra hardness. When the bit turns, the wheels roll around. The teeth strike the rock like dozens of hammers.

The bit is attached to one end of a metal pipe. A motor at the top of the drilling hole makes the pipe spin around. A metal tower, called a derrick, is over the drilling hole. The derrick holds the pipe upright and lets it down into the hole.

Oil-drill bit

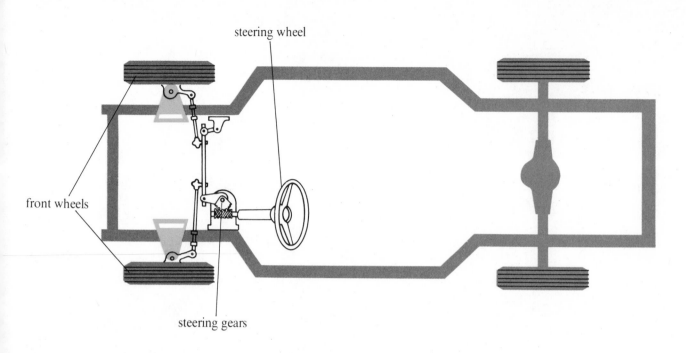

steering wheel

front wheels

steering gears

How does a steering wheel make a car turn?

A steering wheel is connected to a long metal bar, like an axle. It extends down into a metal gearbox in the front of the car. When you turn the steering wheel, you make the bar turn a gear. In many cars the gear is a worm gear. The worm gear turns another gear, which is connected to a lever. The lever is connected to two rods. One rod is attached to the left front wheel, and the other is attached to the right front wheel. When you turn the steering wheel, the gears move the lever. The rods attached to the lever make the car's front wheels turn left or right.

Question:
How does a steering
wheel make a car
turn?
Answer:
How should I know!
Sally Brown

What makes roller skates and skateboards roll easily?

Inside the wheels of roller skates and skateboards are little steel balls called ball bearings. The ball bearings fit into grooves between the wheels and the axles. If there were no ball bearings, the wheels would rub and scrape on the axles. This kind of rubbing and scraping is called friction (FRICK-shun). It makes wheels hard to turn. If wheels are hard to turn, they can't roll fast. Ball bearings reduce friction and make wheels easy to turn. You can reduce friction even more if you squirt a drop of oil on the ball bearings. Bicycles, cars, and many other kinds of machines use bearings and oil or grease to make them run better.

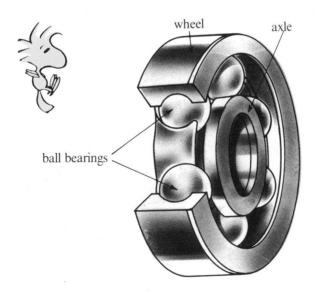

wheel axle

ball bearings

JOE SKATEBOARD!

589

How do the gears on a one-speed bicycle work?

A one-speed bike has just two gears. They are called sprockets. One sprocket is attached to the pedals and one is attached to the rear wheel. A loop of chain goes around the two sprockets. When you pedal, you turn the pedal sprocket. It pushes the chain, which turns the rear-wheel sprocket. And that turns the wheel to make the bike go.

Why do some bicycles have ten speeds?

So that the rider can make the bike go fast without pedaling fast. And so that the rider can go up a hill without straining too hard. When you ride a one-speed bike, some hills are too hard to ride up. You have to get off and push the bike. If you want to go fast on a one-speed bike, you have to pedal very, very fast. And you soon get tired. Three-speed bicycles are better for climbing hills or going fast because they have more gears than one-speed bicycles. More gears mean more possible speeds. Ten-speed bikes are even better.

590

How do the gears on a ten-speed bicycle work?

A ten-speed bike has seven sprockets. Two are attached to the pedals and five are attached to the rear wheel. Each sprocket is a different size. The chain is always looped around one of the pedal sprockets and one of the rear-wheel sprockets. The bike has controls that let you move the chain from one sprocket to another. By doing this, you can get more speed or more forward force—but not both at the same time.

If you wanted to go fast on flat ground, you would put your chain around the large pedal sprocket and the smallest rear-wheel sprocket. This combination would give you the most speed, but the least forward force. You don't need much force to move on flat ground.

If you wanted to go up a hill without pedaling hard, you would need a lot of forward force. So you would put your chain around the small pedal sprocket and the largest rear-wheel sprocket. This combination would give you the most forward force but the least speed. You would go up the hill easily, but slowly.

Ten combinations of rear-wheel and pedal sprockets are possible. That is why the bicycle is called a ten-speed bike. After you have ridden a ten-speed bike for a while, you get to know which combinations are best for the kind of riding you are doing.

What makes springs bouncy?

Springs are bouncy because they have elasticity (ee-lass-TISS-ih-tee). This means you can stretch them or bend them or squeeze them, and they will quickly go back to their original shape when you let go. Rubber bands have elasticity. That's why people often call them elastic bands.

How does a pogo stick help people to jump high?

A pogo stick has a spring inside it. A spring, or any elastic thing, can store energy. When you jump down on a pogo stick, you use energy to squeeze the spring. The spring stores the energy for just a moment, until you start to jump up. Then, the energy in the spring is let out. It gives you an extra boost and helps you to go higher.

In 1976 William Hanrahan kept jumping on a pogo stick for ten hours and one minute. He made 70,076 jumps!

THAT'S THE WAY!

592

Is a diving board a machine?

Yes, a diving board is really a spring. Springs aren't always shaped like a curly piece of wire. Springs can be flat, and they can even be made of wood. Anything that bends without breaking and then snaps back to its original position is a spring. Divers like a springy diving board because it helps them to jump high. When divers jump high, they have time to do fancy tricks in the air before they plunge into the water.

How do a bow and arrow work?

The bow is a spring. When you pull back the string, you bend the bow and put energy into it. When you let go of the string, the energy is let out very suddenly. It gives the arrow a strong, fast push.

An arrow is not very heavy. You could throw it with your hand, as if it were a spear. But it wouldn't go very far. This is because your hand can't push the arrow as fast as the bow does. The faster you push the arrow, the farther it will go.

 Some very strong bows can shoot an arrow more than half a mile (nearly 1 kilometer)!

How does a bathroom scale work?

A bathroom scale uses a spring to measure weight. When you stand on the scale, you cause a bar to pull down on the spring. The spring stretches. The heavier you are, the more it stretches. As the spring stretches, a piece of metal swings down and pushes a second bar. This bar is long and flat and has gear teeth along one edge. It turns a small gear. The small gear turns an axle, which turns a wheel. The wheel has numbers printed on it. These are the numbers that show through the window in the top of the scale. When the wheel stops turning, you see a number under the pointer. This is how much you weigh.

Do all scales have springs?

No. Doctors and nurses weigh people on scales that have no springs. This kind of scale uses a lever to measure weight. The lever works like a seesaw. When you step on the scale, the weight of your body pulls down one side of the lever. The other side of the lever has metal weights. These can slide along bars that have numbers. The doctor or nurse moves the metal weights back and forth along the bars until the lever balances. If a person weighs 82 pounds, for example, the lever will balance when the big weight is on 50 and the small weight is on 32 ($50+32=82$). Doctors and nurses prefer this kind of scale because it is more exact than a bathroom scale.

METAL WEIGHTS

LEVER

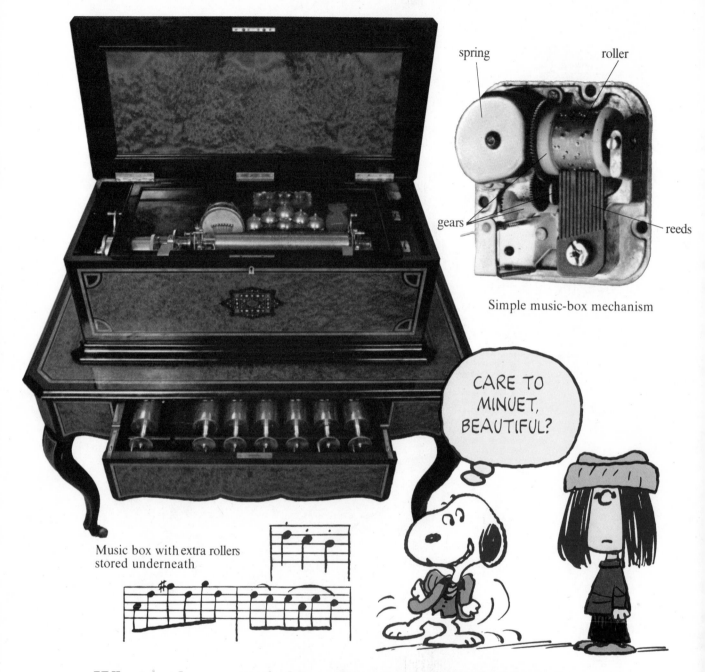

spring

roller

gears

reeds

Simple music-box mechanism

CARE TO MINUET, BEAUTIFUL?

Music box with extra rollers stored underneath

What makes a music box play when you wind it up?

A music box is powered by a spring that works like a motor. This kind of spring is a flat piece of metal rolled up like a spool of ribbon. When you wind up the spring, you are rolling it tight. You are also putting energy into it. When the spring is released, the energy stored in it makes it unwind and turn around in a circle. When the spring turns around, it turns a gear. This gear turns a second gear, which is attached to a roller. The roller has little spikes sticking out of it. When the roller turns, the spikes push aside thin pieces of metal called reeds. The reeds twang like strings of a guitar. And you hear music.

Why does a windup watch tick?

Because it keeps stopping and starting again. A windup watch is powered by the same kind of spring that runs a music box. The spring turns gears, which make the hands go around. If the gears kept turning, without ever stopping, the energy in the spring would escape very fast. And the hands would whirl around too quickly. So something called an escapement (eh-SCAPE-ment) was invented to keep the hands from spinning too fast. Here's how it works.

Inside the watch is a tiny lever. At each end of the lever is a hook. The lever flips back and forth like a seesaw going up and down. Each time the lever flips, one of the hooks catches a tooth on one of the watch's gears. The watch stops for a fraction of a second. Then the hook releases the gear tooth and the watch starts again. Stop and go, stop and go. Tick, tick, tick, tick. Each tick is the sound of a hook letting go of a gear tooth.

 You can *see* your watch stopping and starting.
Just keep your eye on the jerky motion of the second hand!

597

Why is a grandfather clock tall?

A grandfather clock is tall because it needs a lot of room inside for the long clock parts that hang down. Most grandfather clocks have a glass door in the front. You can look in and see the parts—weights, chimes, and a pendulum.

What is a pendulum?

A pendulum is the clock part you see swinging back and forth. It controls how fast the clock runs, just like the escapement in a windup watch. You can make the pendulum longer or shorter. Just loosen a screw and move the pendulum up or down. If you make it longer, the clock will run slower. If you make it shorter, the clock will run faster.

Why do grandfather clocks have to be wound up?

Unless they are wound, they run out of energy. Some clocks have a windup spring—just as a watch does. But grandfather clocks have no windup spring. They get their energy from the weights that hang down behind the pendulum. Each weight pulls on the chain. The chains turn gears inside the top of the clock. As the clock runs, the weights move slowly down. After a while, the weights have to be pulled up again, or else the clock will stop. Winding the clock lifts the weights.

What makes a grandfather clock chime?

Hanging behind the weights on a clock are metal tubes called chimes. They make musical sounds when small hammers in the top of the clock hit them. The gears that turn the clock's hands also make the hammers strike the chimes. Every hour, on the hour, the chimes play a short tune: one bong at one o'clock, two at two o'clock, and all the way up to twelve bongs at noon or midnight.

Grandfathers aren't the only ones who have a clock named after them. Grandmothers do too! A grandmother clock looks just like a grandfather clock, only it's shorter.

599

What makes an alarm clock ring?

A bell. Some clocks have the bell on top of the case. Others have it inside. With many clocks, the metal case itself is the bell. The bell rings when a small hammer or clapper strikes it. The hammer is held down by a hook until the right time comes.

Suppose you set your clock for 7:30. Behind the knob you use to set the alarm is a gear. On it is a special trigger bump. At 7:30 this bump will meet up with a hole in the gear that turns the hour hand. When the bump goes into the hole, the hour-hand gear moves closer to the alarm gear. This movement causes the hook holding the hammer to be pushed out of place. The hammer is released. And . . . Rrrrrriiiiinnnggg! When you shut off the alarm, a hook will hold the hammer still once again.

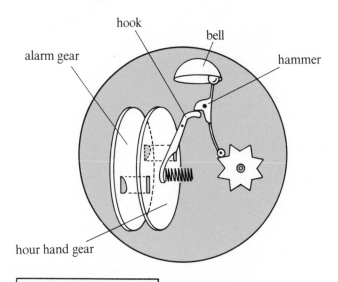

hook

bell

alarm gear

hammer

hour hand gear

How does a toaster know when to pop up?

Inside a toaster is a timer, which is just like a clock. When you push the knob down to start the toaster, you are also winding up the timer. The timer goes ticka-ticka-tick while it's unwinding. When the timer is all unwound, it releases a spring that makes your toast pop up. If you set your toaster to make light toast, then the timer will run fast. If you set it to make dark toast, then the timer will run slowly. Your toast will stay down inside and cook longer. The timer on most toasters works even when the toaster is not plugged in. It does not need electricity to do its job.

How does a key unlock a lock?

Inside a lock are little metal rods called tumblers. Most locks have five tumblers. They are lined up in a row in the top part of the lock. The tumblers poke down into the part of the lock that turns. In this way, they jam the lock so that it can't turn. Suppose you put the right key into a lock. The bumps on the top of the key push the tumblers out of the way. Then you can turn the key and unlock the lock. But suppose you use the wrong key. It will push the tumblers too far or not enough. This is because the bumps on a wrong key are higher or lower than the bumps on the right key. If you use the wrong key, the tumblers will keep jamming the lock so that it won't open.

WOODSTOCK IS RIGHT. IF YOU LIVE IN A NEST YOU DON'T HAVE TO BOTHER ABOUT LOCKS....

tumbler

key

Why was the carpet sweeper invented?

Because of an allergy. Mr. Melville R. Bissell owned a china shop. Unfortunately, he was allergic to straw dust. All the china that arrived at his shop came packed in dusty straw. After he unpacked a shipment of china, he needed to get the dust out of his shop. Otherwise his allergy would bother him. This was back around 1876, before vacuum cleaners were invented. With no vacuum cleaner available, Bissell had to use a broom. But brooms kick dust into the air. For a person who is allergic, straw dust in the air is even worse than straw dust on the floor. So Bissell invented a sweeper with a built-in dustpan. When he cleaned with it, the dust went right into the pan. It never went into the air. Bissell sweepers soon became popular in many parts of the world. They are still used today.

YOU WANNA KNOW WHY THE CARPET SWEEPER WAS INVENTED?... I'LL TELL YOU WHY THE CARPET SWEEPER WAS INVENTED.

Why does a saw make sawdust?

Because a saw works like hundreds of very tiny axes chopping. An ax strikes with great force. It bites big chunks out of a piece of wood. A saw is for making careful, neat cuts in wood, plastic, or metal. Each tooth on a saw blade is like a tiny, sharp ax. When you make a saw go back and forth across what you are cutting, the teeth bite off little chunks. Each little chunk is a piece of sawdust.

❗ The sharpest saws have teeth made of diamonds! ❗

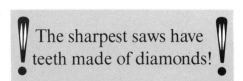

LOOK, IF YOU THINK A DIAMOND RING IS TOO MUCH OF A COMMITMENT, I'LL SETTLE FOR A SAW.

How do furniture makers carve chair legs into fancy shapes?

With a power tool called a lathe. The lathe holds the piece of wood being carved. When the motor is turned on, the wood begins to spin around very fast. While the wood is spinning, the furniture maker presses another tool called a chisel against the wood. The chisel is very sharp. It shaves little pieces off the spinning wood. Chisels come in several shapes for doing different kinds of carving. Lathes can also be used to shape metal.

Why do sharp knives cut better than dull knives?

Because sharp knife blades are thinner than dull knife blades. And because sharp knife blades have a rougher edge than dull knife blades. In order to cut through something tough, such as the skin of a tomato, you need a sharp knife. Tiny teeth, so small you can see them only under a microscope, are all along the edge of a sharp blade (unless it's the blade of a steak knife—then it has large teeth). These teeth bite and tear at the tomato skin. And, because a sharp blade is very thin, it has a very narrow area of tomato skin to push through. The dull blade is wider than a sharp blade. So it has to push through more tomato skin. It also has no little teeth for biting into the skin. So a dull blade can cut only soft things like butter or a slice of white bread.

605

How does a lawn mower cut grass?

With a blade. The most popular type of lawn mower is the rotary power mower. "Rotary" means turning or spinning around. A rotary blade spins like a fan or an airplane propeller. A gasoline or electric motor supplies the energy to spin the blade. When the blade spins, it creates a wind. The spinning blade pulls air up from underneath the mower. It blows the air out a hole in the side or the back of the mower. The moving air makes the grass stand up straight. Then the blade can chop it all off at the same height. The result is a lawn that looks smooth and even.

Does a lawn mower do anything besides cut grass?

Yes. The air pulled in from underneath the mower sucks up leaves. It also sucks up any paper or trash that might be lying around. The blade chops the leaves and trash into tiny pieces. Some mowers collect the grass clippings, leaves, and trash in a bag. Then you can easily throw them away. Other mowers blow all the chopped-up pieces out onto the lawn. Then you have to rake them up.

The biggest lawn mower on record is 60 feet (18 meters) wide. It can mow one acre (less than one hectare) of grass in one minute!

How does a pencil sharpener sharpen pencils?

Inside a hand-cranked sharpener, there are two metal rollers side by side. Sharp ridges, almost like knife blades, stick out from the rollers. These ridges are for shaving little pieces of wood off a pencil. The pencil fits into a space between the two rollers. The space is wide at one end. It comes to a point at the other end. When you turn the crank, the rollers spin. They shave your pencil into the same shape as the space between the two rollers.

How does an electric pencil sharpener work?

Instead of a hand crank, an electric pencil sharpener has a motor. But the rollers that shave the pencil are the same in the electric as in the manual sharpener. When you poke your pencil into the hole of an electric pencil sharpener, the pencil pushes a lever. The lever flips a switch that turns the motor on. The motor makes the rollers spin to sharpen the pencil.

A PENCIL ISN'T REALLY MADE OF LEAD? IT'S HARD TO KNOW WHAT TO BELIEVE IN THESE DAYS....

ROLL WITH THE PUNCHES, SIR!

The "lead" (led) inside a pencil isn't really made of lead. It's mostly a soft, black mineral called graphite!

Who thought of putting an eraser on a pencil?

Mr. Hyman L. Lipman of Philadelphia. And he became rich because of it. Back in the 1850s pencils and erasers had already been invented. But Lipman was the first to think of fastening them together. In 1858 Lipman took out a patent on his idea. His pencils became very popular. With them people didn't have to hunt around for an eraser each time they made a mistake. The fortune Lipman made from his pencils would be worth more than one million dollars in today's money.

What makes a ball-point pen write?

The little ball in the point has something to do with it. When you write, the ball rolls around. As the ball rolls, it picks up ink from a long tube inside the pen. The ball then transfers the ink to the paper.

Before the ball-point pen could be perfected, scientists had to invent a special kind of ink to put in it. Old-fashioned writing ink was too watery. And it leaked out of ball-point pens. So scientists made the ink thicker, like syrup. Then it didn't leak.

Ball-point pens were invented as long ago as 1888. Yet people didn't use them much until the 1950s.

IN 1880 THE BOYS AT THE AGENCY WEREN'T ON THE BALL! HEE HEE HEE!

608

Who invented the printing press?

A German named Johannes Gutenberg (yo-HAHN-us GOOT-un-berg) around the year 1440. Before that, Europeans carved wood blocks and pressed them against paper or copied books by hand. Gutenberg's press used a separate piece of metal type for each letter. The pieces of type could be moved around to form different words. Once the type was put in order, the printer inked it. Then he placed a piece of paper over it and turned a giant-sized screw. This pressed a big wooden block against the paper. In that way the ink left its mark on the paper.

Johannes Gutenberg removes a printed page from his press.

609

Some modern printing presses are bigger than a bus.
And they use whole truckloads of paper and ink!

How do modern books get printed?

The greatest advances in printing have been made in the methods of preparing the type for the press. Computers, photography, and even laser beams are used today. For printing large numbers of newspapers, magazines, and books quickly, very big automatic presses are used. The printer just pushes some buttons. Then the press prints several thousand copies of a newspaper in an hour. But modern printing presses are still based on Gutenberg's idea, though they are much bigger and faster than the old-fashioned presses.

This is my new typewriter.

It has many typefaces.

IT CAN ALSO cross out mistakes.

How does a typewriter work?

A typewriter has little pieces of metal in the shape of letters, numbers, and other symbols. These press an inky ribbon or tape against a piece of paper. The little pieces of metal are called type. They are attached to levers called typebars. The buttons that you tap with your fingers are called keys. The keys are connected to the typebars by rods and levers. When you push down on a key, a typebar pops up and whacks its piece of type against the inky ribbon. The type makes its mark on the paper.

Most electric typewriters work in a similar way. But the electric motor makes everything work much more quickly and easily.

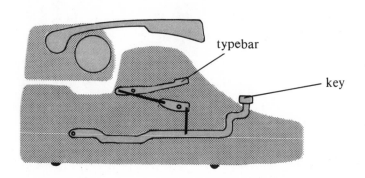
typebar

key

DEAR SIR...

MY SECRETARY ISN'T USED TO AN ELECTRIC TYPEWRITER!

! You probably write about 20 words a minute.
The fastest typists can type 150 to 200 words a minute! !

612

How do Venetian blinds open and close?

A machine inside the Venetian blinds makes them open and close. The machine works with a pulley. A pulley is a wheel that has a groove around the rim to hold a cord or rope.

To make the blinds open or close, you pull a cord. This sets off a chain of events. The cord turns a pulley. The pulley turns a screw. The screw turns a gear. The turning gear changes the slant of the top strip, or slat. This changes the slant of all the slats in the blind. So, more or less light can come in.

I THINK THEY MIGHT LOOK GREAT IN MY DEN.

How do Venetian blinds go up and down?

With a cord and pulleys. To make the blinds go up or down, you pull the cord down or let it go up. This cord is different from the one you pull to open or close Venetian blinds. This cord is threaded through a few pulleys in the heavy rail above the top slat. It also passes down through holes in all the slats to the bottom bar. When you pull down on the cord, it pulls the bottom bar up. And with it, up go as many of the slats as you like.

613

What makes a roller coaster go?

Gravity—the force that makes things fall toward the ground. Roller coasters are powered by gravity, except at the very beginning of the ride. To get started, the roller-coaster cars hook on to a chain. It pulls them to the top of the first hill. The chain can pull the cars because gears connect it to a motor on the ground. When the cars get to the top of the first hill, the hooks let go. Then the cars roll down. They go faster and faster until they reach the bottom. As the cars go up the next hill, they slow down. The same force of gravity that makes the cars go faster when they are coasting down makes them go slower when they are coasting up. Each hill that the cars go up is a little lower than the hill that the cars just rolled down. This is because gravity does not let the cars roll to a place that is as high as the hill they just came from.

What makes an elevator work?

When you step into an elevator and push the button, an electric motor starts up. The motor is in a room at the top of the building. The motor pulls a set of cables that lift the box in which you are riding. This box is called the elevator car. Each cable is a rope made of wires twisted or woven together. The cables run over pulleys attached to the motor. Then the cables go back down the shaft to a counterweight. A counterweight is a weight that balances the car. When the car goes up, the counterweight goes down. When the car goes down, the counterweight goes up. An elevator has an automatic brake that stops the car if it begins to fall.

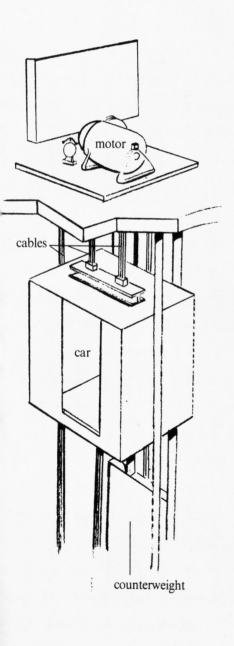

E. G. OTIS

 In 1900 the first escalator was installed by
the Otis Elevator Company at the Paris Exposition.
The machine was moved to the Gimbel Brothers' store in
Philadelphia in 1901, where it was used until 1939.

Where do the steps on an escalator go after they reach the end?

They go underneath the escalator. Then they come out again at the other end. All the steps are hooked together like the links of a chain. Underneath, where you can't see, each step has wheels that run along tracks. These tracks are very much like the tracks that trains run on. An escalator gets its power from a strong electric motor. The motor is connected to a gear that moves a chain. This chain is just like the chain that connects the pedals and rear wheel of a bicycle. But it's a lot bigger. The chain is connected to the escalator's steps. The motor turns the gear, and the gear moves the chain. The moving chain makes the steps move along the tracks.

How does a sewing machine make stitches?

A sewing machine pokes thread through pieces of cloth. Then it ties the thread in loops. In that way, the thread will stay in place and hold the cloth together. When you sew by hand, you use one thread. But when you sew with a sewing machine, you use two threads. One thread comes down from the top of the machine and goes through the eye of the needle. The other thread is in the bottom of the machine. It is wound on a small spool called a bobbin. The needle pushes the top thread down through the cloth. When the needle is down as far as it can go, a hook in the bottom of the machine catches the top thread. The hook wraps the top thread around the bottom thread, and a stitch is made. When the needle goes back up, it pulls the top thread and makes the stitch tight.

618

Elias Howe

Who invented the sewing machine?

Everyone thinks of the American Elias Howe as the inventor of the sewing machine. Howe's machine (patented in 1846) was the most successful. But it was not the first. A sewing machine was patented as long ago as 1790 by Thomas Saint of England. His machine was made for sewing leather. A tool called an awl punched holes in the leather. A needle stitched through the holes.

619

When was the zipper invented?

Whitcomb L. Judson of Chicago took out a patent on the first zipper in 1893. But the early zippers weren't very reliable. Often they would jam, so that they couldn't be opened or closed. Sometimes they would suddenly pop open all by themselves. A person would find himself standing around with his underwear showing. Other people would point and giggle. It was safer to wear clothes with buttons. But then in 1913 Gideon Sundback of Sweden invented an improved zipper that was reliable. Still, zippers didn't really become popular until the 1930s. That's when the leading fashion designers began to use them.

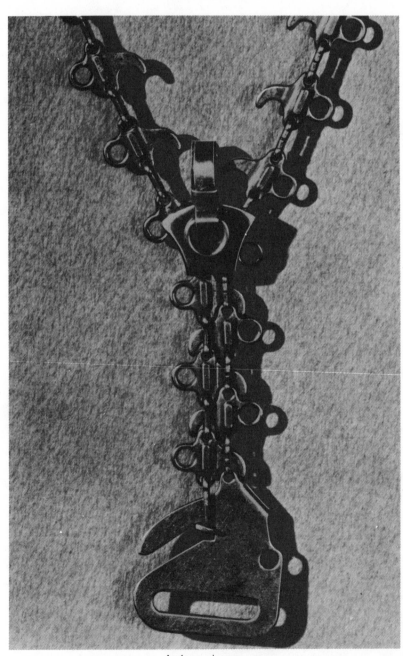

Judson zipper

How does a zipper work?

A zipper has two rows of teeth that lock together when you zip it up. A little bump on the top of each tooth fits into a little hole in the bottom of the tooth above.

The part that you pull up and down is called the slide. Inside it is a Y-shaped track. The two rows of teeth run through this track. Inside the track, the teeth bend and the spaces between them become wider. The wider spaces let the teeth fit together when you pull the slide up. They let the teeth come apart when you pull the slide down. On some zippers, the teeth are made of metal. Other zippers have plastic teeth, and each row of teeth looks like a long, thin spring.

What does a cotton gin do?

A cotton gin is a machine that takes the seeds out of cotton. After the cotton is picked, the seeds have to be taken out. Then the fluffy white fibers can be made into thread, yarn, and cloth. Before Eli Whitney invented the cotton gin in 1793, people had to take out the seeds by hand. This was very slow work. It limited the amount of cotton a farmer could grow and sell. Whitney's cotton gin used a hand crank to turn two rollers. One roller had metal claws to pull the cotton off the seeds. The other roller had bristles to brush the cotton off the claws. Then it could be gathered up. Modern cotton gins are larger and faster than Eli Whitney's. But they are based on his idea.

Cotton gin

ELI WHITNEY

622

Did Eli Whitney invent anything besides the cotton gin?

Yes. Eli Whitney invented a way of making things quickly. It is called mass production.

In the 1700s and before, people built machines one at a time. This process was slow. And no two machines came out exactly alike. Whitney changed all that. He started mass production of guns called muskets. He made batches of musket parts at once. He made all the barrels exactly alike. He made all the triggers exactly alike, and so on. In this way, a factory worker could take one of each part and put together a musket. Other workers could each specialize in making one kind of part. Whitney showed his idea to the United States Government in 1798. He was hired to make 10,000 muskets for the army. Modern factories still use Whitney's idea to make almost anything you can think of.

Workers using mass-produced parts on car assembly line

How did factories make their machines run before engines and motors were developed?

They used water wheels. This meant that factories had to be built close to a fast-flowing stream or river. A water wheel was made of wood. It had paddles or buckets around the rim. Part of the wheel was always in the water. As the stream flowed, water pushed against the paddles or buckets. It made the wheel turn. The wheel was attached to an axle called a drive shaft. Drive shafts were often very large. Some were made from the whole trunk of a tall tree. The drive shaft reached from the water wheel to the inside of the factory. When the water wheel turned, it made the drive shaft run the machines. In many factories, the drive shaft was used to turn other drive shafts. These other drive shafts reached upstairs and downstairs and all through the factory. In that way many machines could run at the same time.

A wedge is a special type of inclined plane. It has two or more surfaces that slope to an edge or a point.

One type of wedge is used to split logs. First the wedge is placed on the end of a log. When someone strikes the wedge with a mallet or hammer, its sides push the log apart. The wedge changes the downward force of the hammer into a sideward force that pushes the log apart. The deeper the wedge goes in, the wider the two halves of the log are pushed apart. Finally the log splits into two pieces. Axes, hatchets, and knives are sharp tools that are shaped like wedges to help them work better. Pins and nails are examples of pointed wedges. The points help the pin or nail go in easier. This is because the material in the way is pushed to the side to let the pin or nail go through. A flat-ended pin or nail would have to push the material ahead of it, instead of to the side, and it would be very hard to make this kind of pin or nail go in.

Some clocks can do a lot more than tell time. Astronomical clocks can show the date, the month, the phases of the moon, and the positions of the planets. Public clocks in some places ring chimes and play music—and even make mechanical figures dance!

Above: Musical clock in Munich, Germany.
Left: Detail showing mechanical figures

A parking meter is really a type of clock. When you put a coin in the slot, the coin drops into a system of levers. The levers figure out how big the coin is. When you turn a knob, a pointer comes into the window to show you how much time you have paid for.

By turning the knob, you also wind the clock inside the meter. If you listen closely, you may be able to hear it ticking. The clock slowly moves the pointer backward to let you know how much time you have left. When your time runs out, the pointer goes to zero—and a red flag pops up in the window.

Every week or so, a worker comes around and unlocks the bottom part of the meter. That's when he collects the money for the local government.

A pulley is a wheel with a groove in the rim. On a bicycle or car wheel, a groove in the rim holds a tire in place. But on a pulley, the groove holds a rope and keeps it from slipping off.

If you hang a pulley from a high place, like a ceiling or a tree limb, you can use it to lift a heavy object easily. With a pulley, you are not using just your muscles to lift. You are also using the weight of your body. As long as the object you are lifting weighs less than you, you can lift it with a single pulley just by attaching it to one end of the rope and pulling down on the other end.

If the object you want to lift is heavier than you, you can lift it if you add more pulleys. For example, if you arrange two double pulleys so that the object you are lifting is supported by four lengths of rope, you can lift a weight four times heavier than yourself.